CONTENTS

ACKNOWLEDGEMENTS

INTRODUCTION

DESMOND L. KHARMAWPHLANG (b. 1964), a collector of Khasi folk stories and a lecturer at North-Eastern Hill University, Shillong, has published two collections of poetry, the bilingual *Touchstone/U Mawshamok* (1988) and *Here* (Writers' Forum, 1992), and is represented in *An Anthology of New Indian English Poetry* (Rupa, New Delhi, 1993). He co-edits the cultural journal *Muses* and the poetry magazine *Lyric*, and has published widely on Khasi folklore. Taking his mother's name in accordance with the Khasis' matrilineal tradition, he is the son of the no

Ka Jingshah Jop!
The Conquest
Y Goresgyniad
Letter from Pahambir
Umiam, August 19
Pictures (for Lisa)
And Some Bangles
The September Song

ROBIN S. NGANGOM (b. 1959), whose poetry will be familiar to readers of *The New Statesman*, is not a Khasi but a Meitei from nearby Manipur, although he has lived in Shillong for many years, and is perhaps the first 'outsider' to use 'the matter of Khasia' in his poetry. A lecturer in English at North-

Eastern Hill University, Shillong, he has published two books of poetry, *Words and the Silence* (Writers Workshop, 1988) and *Time's Crossroads* (Orient Longman, 1994), and appears in *An Anthology of New Indian English Poetry* (Rupa, New Delhi, 1993).

The Strange Affair of Robin S. Ngangom
Teithlyfr
Values
A Poem for Mother

LESLIE HARDINGE PDE (b. 1938) lives in Shillong and is the state of Meghalaya's Labour Commissioner, and director of Employment and Craftsmen Training. He has written five novels, plays, short stories, factual books and articles, and translated into Khasi some of the classics of Indian literature. He is currently working on a translation of Dante's *The Divine Comedy*.

The Mawphlang Sacred Grove

KYNPHAM SINGH NONGKYNRIH (b. 1964) is editor of the English-language daily newspaper *Apphira* and lectures in English at Sankardev College, Shillong. A translator, critic and essayist, in both English and Khasi, he is an authority on Khasi religion, customs and folk tales. His poetry, widely published and anthologised, is collected in two volumes, *Moments* (1992) and *The Sieve* (1992), both from Writers Workshop editions, Calcutta.

Weiking
The Invitation

Cartrefi Prydles yn Shillong
Only My Tenant
The Parking Lot
Only Strange Flowers Have Come to Bloom
Winter Song

GWENETH ALICIA MAWLONG (b. 1969) is a postgraduate student of media-communication in New Delhi, though her home is Shillong in the Khasi Hills. As a singer-songwriter, in both English and Khasi, she is a frequent performer on local and national radio and television. A member of Shillong's Lyric Synthesis performance group, she gives poetry readings and has published in a variety of journals and magazines.

A Lady
Rendezvous
For Jerilee
To the Hills I Know

KHASI MUSIC

BIOGRAPHIES OF THE MUSICIANS

ACKNOWLEDGEMENTS

Some of the poems in this anthology first appeared in *Lyric* (Shillong), *The New Welsh Review* (Cardiff), *Swagmag* (Swansea), or were broadcast on All India Radio and Doordarshan, the national television station, or were published in *An Anthology of New Indian English Poetry* (1993) and the individual collections of Desmond Kharmawphlang (*U Mawshamok/Touchstone*, 1988; *Here*, 1992), Robin S. Ngangom (*Words and the Silence*, 1988; *Time's Crossroads*, 1994) and Kynpham Singh Nongkynrih (*Moments*, 1992).

Thanks are due to Dafydd Rowlands for translating three of the poems into Welsh; to Andy Dark for the cover; to Kevin Thomas and Sarah Stone of the Welsh Academy; to the staff at Gwasg Gomer; to the staff of the UK Year of Literature and Writing 1995, particularly Sean Doran and Derek Cobley; and, above all, to Ruth Stevenson for organising the tour: *diolch o galon, gyfeillion.*

INTRODUCTION

A paleface, godsent young man
entered once our mistwoven hills,
brought us letters, literature and the Bible.
He was a Welshman.
The Tommies, however, brought spite,
spattered the ferns with our fathers' blood
and spoke to us in gunfire tones.

(Almond Dean Syiem)

The founding father of their written language and literature, the Khasis readily acknowledge, was a Welshman. In 1840 a Montgomeryshire miller by the name of Thomas Jones (1810-1849) travelled some thirteen thousand ocean miles to establish in the mountains of north-east India the Calvinistic Methodists' Mission to the Khasis, which would become the biggest overseas venture ever sustained by the Welsh people.

Though the missionaries left India a quarter of a century ago, the Welsh legacy in the Khasi Jaintia Hills, to give them their full name, is like the bloom of *cawl cennin* drifting from the missionary kitchen through the whole of the Khasi house. While the Khasis remember the Welsh—more with affection, I think, for the good the missionaries did them, than regret for any Puritanical heavy-handedness—it is curious and sad that in Wales the Khasi connection has dropped into the great dark sack of national forgetting.

Having visited the Khasi Hills, to write a book and make a film about the Mission, I was keen to develop the relationship between our two peoples on a more secular level.   I wanted to bring a party of Khasi writers and musicians to Wales, and went with this impractical dream to the organisers of Swansea's

U.K. Year of Literature and Writing 1995. To my delight, Sean Doran and company had no difficulty in recognising the significance of inviting a group of prominent Khasi artists to encounter at first hand the country whose missionaries had given them the beginnings of a literature, while at the same time exposing Welsh audiences to the poetry, stories and music of a culture entirely new to them—but with which they were intimately connected. It would be a difficult and costly project, but the Year of Literature, *khublei shibun*, embraced it wholeheartedly.

This anthology of contemporary Khasi writing, the first to appear in the West, has been published to coincide with and accompany the June-July '95 tour of Wales by five writers from the Khasi Hills and three musicians. Khasi music is visited elsewhere in this volume; my purpose here is to set the writers in their cultural context.

Of course, the Khasis were weaving stories and minting songs long before the Bible-thumping, hymn-crazy Welsh arrived on the scene. The richness of their oral and folk traditions is still to be savoured in the isolated hutments of gorge and jungle where the most popular form of entertainment is a long story-telling session round the fire, with extemporised musical accompaniment.

In the jungle village of Pahambir I was privileged to see a shamanistic poet in action. This spindly old fellow, who must have been in his nineties, sank himself into a trance; then, rolling an egg round in his hand, he launched into a gripping narrative about the sun and the moon and the creatures of the earth, his voice rising and falling as if in the throes of some oriental blues. Although I understood not a word of his story, its music and the sacramental atavism of the occasion sent all the rivers of Khasia coursing down my spine. This was poetry, the marrow, bone and flesh of it; here in all his knobbly, bardic majesty, was the kind of poet that we in Wales could only write history books about, a functioning remembrancer of the tribe.

The maturity and power of this oral tradition was to be heard, had the colonisers an ear for it, at least a century and a half earlier—in, for instance, this song of lamentation by the wife of a general in Tirot Singh's army of resistance during the Anglo-Khasi War (1829-1833):

> O the anguish I have suffered
> Because of Mon's obsession.
> No more does he care for the family,
> And the world to me is sad and dreary.
> The thatch is a shambles,
> Our clothes are in tatters,
> For the master is away from here.
> Cold the wind that moans
> Around the hut of Mon,
> Furious its moan, rageful its moan
> Through these cracked walls.
> The children cry in fear,
> The women moan in tears.
> Where is there not woe,
> Where is there not wailing?

The Khasis, who lost that war, were among the last people in the subcontinent to submit to the imperialists' might.

The Welsh, arriving in the Khasi Hills eight years after the end of the war, were part of that classic imperialist chronology succinctly defined by General Sir Charles Napier, the conqueror of Sindh: "a good thrashing first and great kindness afterwards". In addition to converting thousands of Khasis and their compatriot Jaintias to Christianity, they opened the first schools, they founded the first dispensaries and hospitals, and ran medical care programmes; they recognised in the Khasis a

11

small people with an ancient language who were confronted with powerful new forces that threatened to sweep their culture away. No-one can deny that as the Welsh, in their 'kindness', built they also destroyed. Even Christians, who today constitute about half of the Khasi Jaintia population of one million, acknowledge the harm that was done to the Khasi way of life by boxing converts away in mission compounds and attacking every manifestation of tribal culture—from musical instruments and rice beer to traditional sports and personal names. What perhaps the Khasis do not realise is that the Welsh, in the name of Reformed Christianity, had recently subjected their own civilisation to almost identical prohibitions. In the ensuing upheavals, both societies re-made themselves. What survived the cultural attrition was, in both cases, the one tool that was vital to the negotiation of a future, the native language.

When Thomas Jones and his young wife Anne arrived in Cherrapunji, the gorge-encircled settlement that is notorious as the wettest place in the world, the task that faced them seemed enormous. "Go home, Jones," advised a British official. "You may as well try to instruct the monkeys in that tree as attempt to teach these people."

Skilled at home in Aberriw as miller, cooper, wheelwright, carpenter, farm worker, he addressed himself briskly to the practicalities of the situation, and made himself useful to the Khasis by passing on his expertise in the mechanical arts. At the same time, he was learning Khasi and using Welsh orthography to cast the language in written form. Although earlier attempts to reduce Khasi to the complex Bengali script had proved unsuccessful, most authorities continued to advocate perseverance with it. Thomas Jones, as tenacious as he was inventive, pressed on with the Roman script, devising a form for the written language that, with some adaptations, still holds good today.

Early in 1842 he published for use in the Mission's first three schools his translations of *Rhodd Mam* (A Mother's Gift) and his *First Khasi Reader*. These, the first publications in the tribe's own language, mark the modest beginnings of Khasi literature.

After eighteen months alone in the field the Joneses were joined by three new workers from Wales, and by 1846 the Mission had notched up its first converts. But Thomas Jones's sojourn among the Khasis came to an abrupt end when he was run out of the region by one Harry Inglis and a posse of hired thugs after he had protested through the courts and in person against the oppressive consequences of Inglis's monopolisation of most of the economic activity in the southern Hills. He caught malaria as he fled through the jungle, and died in September 1849 in Calcutta. His gravestone there describes him in dazzling marble as "The Founding Father of the Khasi Alphabets and Literature".

Thomas Jones is not indisputably 'the father of Khasi literature'. There are some who feel that this title belongs more properly to Dr. John Roberts, a former Corris quarryman who came to the Hills in 1871. Like most missionaries, Roberts busied himself with religious texts, but he also introduced Khasi readers to a wide range of poetry, folklore, oral tales, country proverbs and general knowledge which had little or no Christian intent. His translations ranged from *Spectator* essays to Longfellow's "The Psalm of Life" and the Felicia Hemans swashbuckler "Casabianca": "The boy stood on the burning deck,/Whence all but him had fled . . ." If the missionaries were dismissive of Khasi music, they were more responsive to traditional Khasi wordcraft, not least, of course, because the collection and publication of Khasi fables and gnomic *phawars* (epigrammatic couplets) helped popularise their Bible-centred literacy programme.

The most famous of John Roberts' adaptations is his Khasi version of "Hen Wlad Fy Nhadau". As "Ri Khasi" (Khasi

Land) it became the Khasi people's national anthem, although they've had to be choosy as to which of his occasionally imperialistic verses they sing today.

Just as Welsh literature was overwhelmingly religious and didactic for two or three hundred years after the translation of the bible, so, for the first forty years, was Khasi literature almost exclusively Christian and moralistic in character. Other works by Thomas Jones include translations of *Yr Hyfforddwr* (a scriptural catechism), the *Gospel of Matthew*, and a collection of hymns, some of which he composed himself. Early translations from the pens of his successors include *Rhodd Tad* (A Father's Gift), *Tyred at Iesu* (Come to Jesus), Watts's *Scripture History*, *Pilgrim's Progress* and *Hanes Mari Jones*. Naturally, their chief literary endeavour was the translation of the bible. In 1891 John Roberts, who alone translated twenty-three books of the *Old Testament*, had the satisfaction of seeing the complete bible pass through the press. That bible, like our own William Morgan version, set a standard of literary excellence for poets and writers for generations to come. Because Cherrapunji was the missionaries' home base in the Hills, it was the speech of Cherra, *Ka Ktien Sohra*, that established itself as literary touchstone and chief of the eleven Khasi dialects.

These prolific litterateurs were assisted in their labours not only by their spouses but by native members of the Church whom they would call upon for advice. However, it was not until 1888 that the first ever book of Khasi poetry appeared, Sheikh Muhamad Amjad Ali's *Ka Myntoi* (Profit)—and that collection, as the author's name implies, was not by a native-born Khasi. Ali was born to a Muslim family in the town of Sylhet, in what is now Bangladesh, although he spent most of his life among the Khasis and identified strongly with their cause—sometimes, at any rate: in one poem he calls on the Khasis to revolt against their flirtation with an alien religion and their slavish dependence on the British; in another, he

14

eulogises the Brits for painting much of the world pink, and invites them to carry on the good work. No doubt Ali, like Whitman, contained multitudes; he certainly perplexed the missionaries who, monopolising the literary scene, did their best to ignore him.

There was no ignoring the cultural revival, at the turn of the century, of which Ali was a precursor. Here, for the first time, was a coherent and purposeful challenge to the influence of Christianity and the missionaries' sway over intellectual and cultural affairs. It was led by the erudite Jeebon Roy, pioneer of secular Khasi literature, who founded an organisation called the Seng Khasi. Still active nearly a century later, the Seng Khasi exists to promote the indigenous faith and culture and to combat the newer religion's 'alien' cultural forms—which include today the happy-clappy schmaltz of American evangelism.

Some of the movement's leading writers, notably Rabon Singh and Radhon Singh Berry, were disenchanted Christians who had abandoned the faith. The one-time mission teacher Rabon Singh, who complains in one poem that thanks to the Christian taboo on alcohol he cannot drink "even a bottle of rice beer/To wish one another good health", renounced Christianity soon after he had been deputed to accompany the Welsh MP Sir J. Herbert Roberts and entourage on a tour of the Hills. The patronising and dismissive attitudes expressed towards Khasi culture by both visitors and missionaries disgusted him.

The proudly Khasi stance adopted by such authors encouraged Christian writers to be more celebratory of their own culture. Soso Tham (1873-1940), a Presbyterian by birth and a pupil of Dr. John Roberts, is accounted the greatest of all Khasi poets. A schoolteacher and lawyer, Soso Tham published two ground-breaking volumes of poetry which, for the first time in Khasi verse, touch on erotic, social and political themes, and sing of everyday life. He attacks the self-forgetful materialism of the present and calls on his compatriots to remember a golden age when the Khasis were at one with each other and the natural world. He laments his contemporaries' ignorance of their own tribal religion, democracy, arts and customs. "We look for knowledge all round the world, but of our own we know nothing," he said, blaming British influence for the low esteem in which Khasis now held their traditional culture. Yet, in the preface to one of his books, he paid sincere tribute to the Mission: "How grateful we are to the Welsh Mission for all it has done. The whole country must think about this. Whose kingdoms are ours? Whose citizens are we? What have the Syiems [native chiefs] and the Khasi states done to drive away darkness? . . . The Mission has led the way; like a tusker, it has trampled down all difficulties without counting the cost; it has poured forth its own wealth and the best of its people for a hundred years . . . "

While the Welsh are often thanked for blazing the literary trail, their influence, which has yet to be analysed by someone familiar with both languages and both traditions, has not always been beneficial. The Welsh in the Khasi Hills wrote primarily to propagandise the Christian faith and way of life, setting an example in worthy moralising which has tainted much that has been written up to the present. The early missionaries were, after all, products of one of the least creative periods in Welsh literary history; this might account to some extent for the view of literature as 'moral uplift' that predominated for at least fifty years after their arrival.

Thomas Jones's contemporary Mary Lewis and later Dr. John Roberts furnished the Khasis with an influential but narrow model of the novel in texts such as *Pilgrim's Progress* and extended reworkings of the biblical stories of Moses and Joseph, with their characters reduced to uncomplicated, static

16

'types' engaged in simple plots based invariably on the ultimate triumph of bright-eyed probity and righteousness over the doomy machinations of evil.

The showy respectability of Welsh Presbyterianism, seeping through to aspiring Khasi writers from the schools, the media and developing institutions, inhibited many authors from tackling some of the psychological and social difficulties of contemporary life. There were powerful voices raised against modern fiction, the evangelist Seint Singh, for instance, declaring in 1934: "We should not give [novels] to young people who are really young mentally, because these will doubtlessly spoil them. We have seen in the whole world that persons who delight in novels do not care anything about the preciousness of their life, and finally ruin themselves in immorality." Hardly an encouragement to a questing young novelist to take up her pen and write.

In the 1960s a new generation of writers shrugged off these stifling prescriptions and began to tackle contemporary social and sexual themes with an uncompromising directness. Chief among them is the novelist Leslie Hardinge Pde. His books, controversial at first, soon caught the popular imagination and were eventually deemed sufficiently 'respectable' to be the subject of a doctoral thesis at the university.

The Khasis, possibly half of whom are literate, have a deep-seated love of good story-telling. A novelist of L.H. Pde's standing can expect to sell 2,000 copies of a new work within two months of publication; some of his titles are into fourth editions, and most of his books, passed eagerly from hand to hand, will have many readers.

The poet of the printed page, as even Soso Tham was obliged to acknowledge, has by contrast a much smaller readership. "This," says Kynpham Singh Nongkynrih, "is because we are fundamentally a story-telling people, not a poetry-writing people." It may also have something to do with

17

the neo-Victorian windiness of much that passes itself off as 'modern' verse, and routinely scoops the state literary awards. This tensionless whimsy, full of dancing daffodils and cuckoos afar, offers at best a chocolate box view of the tribal past and has virtually nothing to say about the agonising dilemmas of the present.

A sad consequence of Khasi poetry's apparent retreat into quaint irrelevance is that many of a talented younger generation, who cut their teeth on Lorca, Seferis, Arghezi, Neruda and the hard-edged modernists of the Third World, have abandoned their native language as a creative medium and taken to English, contributing thereby to 'Anglo-Khasi literature' (yes, the Khasis too have a hyphenated offshoot of the native oak!). Their commitment to the survival of their language and culture is not in question; indeed, it was movingly in evidence at a packed and attentive poetry reading I attended in Shillong, the troubled capital of the state of Meghalaya which the Khasi Jaintias share with their neighbours the Garos. It is simply, I was told, that they wish to dissociate themselves from the daffs and cuckoos of "the old fogeys", and to appeal through newspapers, the radio and Indian publications to a wider public. Another reason for writing in English is hinted at in one of Desmond Kharmawphlang's poems:

> My burdensome English learning
> assails me, and the tomb it has become
> laughs and cackles without end.
> Hiding under dark cloaks of
> my alien patrons, I was taught to be ashamed
> of my own.

It is a painful fact of literary life for certain young writers that although Khasi is their everyday medium, they are not sufficiently confident in the language to make poems in it. This real or imagined incapacity is largely the fault of an education system which obliges secondary school pupils to abandon their native tongue and matriculate in English.

Perhaps in some cases 'the English phase' is temporary and amounts to a purging of clutter before a return to linguistic first positions. But whether writing in Khasi or English, or alternating fluently between both languages, the latest generation of writers from the Khasi Hills prove themselves worthy successors to Soso Tham, to say nothing of Thomas Jones.

DESMOND L. KHARMAWPHLANG

KA JINGSHAH JOP!

Ngam ju ngiah ban kren shaphang
ka shnong lajong.
Ha ka por lyiur, ka bneng ka pun
ka sieb da u slap bym pat kla.

Poi ka tlang, bad ka sngi bajem ka doh
ia ki lum bajar jar bad ia
ki lieng-phohsniew ha ki nan.
Hyndai ki rangbah ki klan sha shiliang
ka Surma ban khaii,
ban lam sha la iing ia ki kynthei
ki ban sumar ia u symbai jongki.

Hadlen dohlieh u wan ryngkat bad
u kuli, ka pisa-snam, bad ka niam.
Suki, ka jingshah jop ha ki jingriew
ki suloi ka la sdang.

Kynsan kynsan, leit noh u dohlieh.
Don biang ka jingsuk bad ka
jingiewbih ki sla jhieh.

Hynrei ha ka at ka them jong ka por
wan kito na rithor shit lynga, na
kylleng sawdong.

Pha ka Ri shahjop, katno
ki ieit ia 'Dew sboh jong pha,
ia ki khun ba la Mong jong pha.

Ong uwei na ki ha nga: "Phi tip
ka shnong jongphi ka dei shisha
ka metropolitan city".

21

THE CONQUEST

I never get tired of talking about my
hometown.
In summer the sky is pregnant,
swollen with unborn rain.

Winter arrives, with a tepid sun
touching the frozen hills, the dream-
boats on lakes.

Long ago, the men went beyond the
Surma
to trade, to bring home women
to nurture their seed.

Later came the British
with gifts of bullets, blood-money
and religion.
A steady conquest to the sound of
guns began.

Quite suddenly, the British left.
There was peace, the sweet
smell of wet leaves again.

But in the wavering walk of time
there came those from the sweltering
plains,
from everywhere.

You stricken Land, how they love
your teeming soil, your bruised children.
One of them told me, "You know,
yours is a truly metropolitan city".

(translation by the author)

22

Y GORESGYNIAD

Ni fyddaf byth yn blino siarad am y
dref sy'n gartref im.
Yn yr haf mae'r wybren yn feichiog,
chwyddedig gan law heb ei eni.

Daw'r gaeaf, a haul claear
yn cyffwrdd â'r bryniau rhynllyd, y lledrith –
gychod ar lynnoedd.

Ers talwm, aeth y dynion y tu draw i
Surma
i fasnachu, a gludo adref wragedd
i feithrin eu had.

Yn ddiweddarach daeth y Prydeinwyr
ag anrhegion o fwledi, arian-gwaed
a chrefydd.
Goresgyniad diwyd i gyfeiliant
gynnau a ddrechreuodd.

Yn hollol sydyn, ymadawodd y Prydeinwyr.
Tangnefedd a fu, a melys
eto sawr lleithder y dail.

Ond gyda threigl anwadal amser
fe ddaethon'nhw o'r chwyslyd
wastadeddau,
o bobman.

Di Wlad luddedig, fel y carant
dy bridd toreithiog, dy blant ysig.
Un ohonynt a ddywedodd wrthyf: "Wyddost ti,
metropolitan yn wir eich dinas chi."

(cyfieithiad gan Dafydd Rowlands)

23

LETTER FROM PAHAMBIR

At sundown we set out in a car,
    past silent, dark huts,
cicadas buzzing the dusk.

We have left the church far behind,
    glowing strangely in pallid
arrogance, through the dust kicked up
    by our passing.

Village curs turn quarrelsome
    as we city men await
the verdict of reception, smoking uneasily
    outside the village Chief's abode.

"We come," I plead, "to learn, not to teach.
    We come with longing, we are the
forgetful generation, our hearts tapping
    a rhythm spawned in shame, a shame
that splits our present from our past.
    We have suckled for so long
on a wisdom of falsehood—we are ourselves
    our own worst enemies."

A fire dances crazily, throwing
    shadows on the hard mud floor, and good
laughter swells like moonlight.
    Someone breaks out in song
and hardened feet tap unsteady punctuations
    around the weird tune.
Voices intone, hands fashion leaf plates
    to hold food for the men
from the big city. I shove more brushwood
    into the fire.

U Di squats on the floor,
   gnarled hands extended, hooded eyes
stealing tiny lights from the fire.
   "See this *diplin*, spattered with
good red mud? Have stored centuries
   of prayers for harvest, a hunt . . .
Our bellies understand hunger, our hands
   are shaped by it. It is black, as only
good smoke can make it; it has
   told my children stories for
countless years now. So wait for the night
   to grow, and endure our
       difficult ways."

U Di strips to loincloth, and bares
   a hunched back, scarred like
a honing stone, upon which hungry
   blades lick like tongues.

With trembling voice, he gazes blindly
   at the night, tension cording his
throat, like vines tying everything
   into a knot of one race of skin
and blood, chanting the songs.

The stories burn our memories like
   a distant meteor searing
the unnamed gloom; by their light I examine
   the great hurt I carry in my soul
for having denied my own.

UMIAM, AUGUST 19

Stones, scattered in the shallows
  around my feet, describing
    tales on the shore.

    Cicadas pierce the air,
drowning the energy of coal trucks
    far away; the gathering clouds
watch mutely this contest of wills.

Down at the lake's edge
  water darkens like an angry secret,
and into its fold I drop a stone.

    Suddenly, like a storm
of heartbreaks, the rains lash,
    and everyone is strangely happy.

PICTURES (for Lisa)

    Sky, speckled with birds,
soaks up dark red wine,
    and lovingly a voice calls.

The kettle spits and splutters;
    outside, the blades wave in morning air.
Sipping scalding tea, I sit back
    and brood: in last night's dream
relatives, long dead, passed slowly through . . .
    But the dead are always gentle.

Lightning is happily licking the clouds,
and a light drizzle falls.
Your hair is wet, damp clothes
delicately sculpt your body.

It amazes me how my defences crumble
into the indentation in your left cheek.

AND SOME BANGLES

I do not know what you're trying to say.
You are hidden, yet sometimes
bigger than the world. You are
nowhere, lost in endless centuries
of man's pride, man's wars,
but still you are soft
in the habitation of his flesh.

I confess, I don't know you. You're
elusive, a hair's-breadth
away from the litany of living,
lugubrious, sad.

I have seen you sold
on the streets, in lanes and
bylanes where shadows do combat
in slow motion, in whispered sins;
then again, with infinite poise,
you carry the dream further,
pumping passion, killing, with smiles,
some thousand men in a matinee show.

I have seen you dancing along
Bombay's Marine Drive
whooping uncontrollably
in a marriage procession, your ample bosom
delectable. Then again, I see it
mauled by a grunting savage
on a cold railway platform far east –
the scavenger crows cawing, flying away.

I have seen you prostrate before
angry gods and angier men—do you
crave beatings so? Ah, girl,
child, woman, skilful performer
in an uncertain world, who are you
to open and close at will
the frontiers of reasoning? That man
had written you off
in a blazing orgy of flames in your
kitchen, and an entire university
rested on holiday. Yet you pour
your man's liquor every evening
and smile when he boasts
or rises to urinate jerkily. You endure
his baldness, his paunch.

Your past flew away
with the seasons, didn't it, and your
learning sits ugly, predator-like,
to haunt you in nightmares
of a remembered marriage, unresolved,
after all the mustard and jasmine
had grown tasteless.

Your hands are adept at making
dung balls for fuel, and the child
rocks easy in them. Your name
is carried across the country to
champion barren lands and hovels.
Do you understand the magic medicine
of two children in a lifetime?

I have seen you cry
over a slain husband, son or
brother. Will you flay your
skin grimly and mutely stand
to contend with ghosts and errors?

That's suffering for you!

See that man? He has made
a hasty bundle of your life.
You were kind, caring,
you were pliant and you
smiled, still, as he burst beastlike
and stupidly drooled.

Yesterday, painters were
slashing you like little boys armed
with fun and colours, while poets
wildly fingered your flighty substance,
gloating in secret. What does it
matter if that man a long time ago
called you a two-bit whore?
You merely smile
your incredible smile.

Girl-child-woman, tell me,
do you dream?

29

THE SEPTEMBER SONG

The streets,
dotted with men in green,
policemen,
arsonists and
miscreants,
growing like unwanted sores,
sigh under the burden
of violence.

Paralysis sets in with curfew,
and the ominous lull
trickles painfully—
a cold shadow on the
edge of your being—the
metallic government voice drags in despair,
"Curfew is relaxed for two
hours"—and
people go wild,
cars wilder,
in an instant
pavements become stalls,
pictures of a mad fair.

The bustle makes no
difference to the beggar woman
who sits on a pavement,
without name, community,
past, future or politics.

During curfew hours, she
and street dogs rule
the deserted streets.

Peace eludes all,
and voices are loudest
of those who speak
of stones, bullets, knives, fire.

And the two lives snuffed
out in this storm of blood
lie unmourned by alien skies.

In the distance, a streak of
lightning tears the sky
in two.

THE STRANGE AFFAIR OF ROBIN S. NGANGOM

Not once can I say
I am the captain
behind this wheel of fire.

I remember misplacing
a bronze bell
somewhere, sometime.
I left behind many untended hearths.
Rushing back I discovered
something had changed me.

I can say
I am this or that,
that I envied the character
of water and stone.
As a boy I was made a sheep,
now I am enchanted into a goat
that the townspeople
enjoy driving to the square
with a marigold garland
between my horns.

At twenty-four
I invited myself to Bohemia.
The kingdom of Art,
where people never grow old,
was my affable neighbour.

Moved by curiosity,
I found myself lingering
at backstages, where painted girls

and poor blind boys
came to do their parts.
In the evenings now,
I often mix my drink with despair.
Love, of course, made me entirely useless.

This is the story of my people.
We sowed suspicion in the fields.
Hatred sprang and razed the crops.
Now they go to gloating neighbours,
begging bowls in hand,
fingers pointed at each other.
Their incessant bickering
muffles all pity.

Our intentions are clear.
Slash and burn,
let fire erase all traces,
so that suspicion cannot write
our murderous history.
Somewhere inside the labyrinth
we met, locked horns, and
went our separate ways.
Our past, we believe, is pristine
even as we reaped heads and took slaves.
When we re-write make-believe history
with malicious intent,
memory burns on a short fuse.

As boys return to Christmas,
escorted by suspicion and fear,
they take a circuitous route
to outwit an enemy
who will revel too much in the birth
of a merciful son. When these boys

reach home, their dreams will come
dressed in red.
Hands filled with love,
I touched your healing breasts.
Like the beaten-up past
scars appeared on your body.
I ask, who branded the moonskin of my love?
Who used you like a toy doll?
And my hands came back to me
stigmatised with guilt.

When I turn with a heavy heart
towards my flaming country,
the hills, woman, scream your name.
Soldiers with black scarves
like mime artists
turn them in seconds into shrouds.
For the trucks carrying
the appliances of death and devastation,
for the eager rescuer in his armoured car,
for the first visitor to the fabled homeland,
the graves of youths who died in turmoil
are the only milestones to the city.
But the hills lie draped in mist.
Instead of the musk of your being
I inhale the acrid smoke
of gelignite and pyres.

With cargoes of sand and mortar
Mammon came to inspect the city.
He cut down the remaining trees
and carried them away
like cadavers for dissection.
Morning papers like watered-down milk
sell the same bland items:

rape, extortion, ambushes, confessions,
embezzlement, vendetta, sales,
marriages, the usual.

There is talk on the streets,
in dark corners, in homes, words
caught by the ears of a restaurant.
We honour the unvarying certainty,
and pay routine homage to silence.
Everyone has correctly identified
the enemy of the people.
He wears a new face each morning,
and freedom is asking yourself
if you are free, day after sullen day.

Uprightness is not caressing anything publicly,
uprightness is not drinking,
uprightness is contributing generously to a new faith
to buy guns for unleashing ideological horror,
uprightness is milking the state
and when you can lift no more
to start burgling each other
so that we can become paragons of thievery,
uprightness is saying that
our women cannot expose their legs,
uprightness is not whispering
even a solitary word of love
so that it will not be mistaken
for unpardonable obscenity.

Nothing is certain:
oil
lentils
vegetables

food for babies
transport
the outside world.
Even
fire water and air
are slowly becoming commodities.

Patriotism is the need of the hour.
Patriotism is preaching secession
and mourning our merger with a nation,
patriotism is honouring martyrs
who died in confusion,
patriotism is declaring we should
preserve native customs and traditions,
our literature and performing arts,
and inflicting them on hapless peoples,
patriotism is admiring
the youth who fondles grenades,
patriotism is proclaiming all men are brothers
and secretly depriving my brother,
patriotism is playing the music of guns
to the child in the womb.

Stones speak, the hills speak
when we finally fall silent.
History, hunch-backed friend,
why do we fear you,
why do we love, hate, lie,
conceal, merely to enact you
in the coarse theatre of time?

Today, I stand alone and acknowledge
the left-handed gift of a man
without a woman, and

a tiny land bound by fire.
Slave to an unexamined life,
all that I've done
I've accomplished blindfolded:
love, fear, anger, and old despair.

The penitent year wears sackcloth
and pours ashen leaves on its head,
the sky's dress is in shreds.
When stars appear, they hold up the sky
like nuts and bolts so that
the firmament will not fall.
But we who sleep under these stars
wish bitter dreams to one another.
Love is also a forgotten word.
The ability to suffer, and the ability
to inflict the utmost hurt
on the person you love most,
this is how I've known it.

The festival of lights
happened during childhood.
Today, I'm again with widows
who cannot light lamps anymore.

Maybe the land is tired
of being suckled on blood,
maybe there is no peace
between the farmer and his fields,
maybe all men everywhere
are tired of being men,
maybe no-one seeks justice,
maybe we have finally accepted
the reality of death.

My love, how can I explain
that I abominate laws
which punish a man for his past,
only the night seems to understand
that we must bear it again.

When I am gone
I would leave you these:
a life without mirrors,
the blue ode between pines
and the winter sky, the
secret understanding of
roots and the earth.

But where can one run from the homeland,
where can I flee from your love?
They have become pursuing prisons
which hold the man
with criminal words.

TEITHLYFR
(ar ôl Derek Walcott)

Yn y gaeaf, mae cytiau'n ymgwtsho
yn oerni tiriogaeth ffiwdal,
ac fe ddeil gwerinwr y bryniau
i eistedd, llafurio a breuddwydio
heb amgyffred y cynnydd gwenwynig
sydd yn nghoncrit hagr a threfydd gorbrysur
y trefedigaethau Gogledd-Ddwyrain hyn.
Rhwygwch yn fân eich pasports
pan ddewch chi yma.

Yma brodorion mor drachwantus â dinasyddion
India annibynnol,
merched i'w llogi wrth y concwistador-werthwr:
byw a wnawn fel Babel o lwythau lliwgar
yn gwerthu diwylliant brodorol
yn y bydoedd hyn y dewch ar eu traws
yn Encyclopaedia Britannica
a llyfrynnau twristiaid.
A phan fydd y tyrchwr
o'r gwastadeddau celyd
yn ystyried ein bryniau hygoelus
dylai gofio
y gwnawn ninnau sy'n ymddangos yn anwar
frathu hefyd y llaw sy'n porthi.

VALUES

You say that for all my acquired learning
a mechanic, a clerk, class III officers
earn much more than me. Perhaps.
It is no use. It is futile.
O smart man with smart dreams,
you have all the answers.

It is all true.
I'm not a newly-rich upstart.
I cannot parade gaudy colours,
crude baubles, before your swinish eyes.
I have not inherited
a sleek collaboration motorcar
to cruise on your slimy roads

built by your inviolate engineers;
nor a bungalow of very bad architecture
with easy money, ill-gotten gains.
I have not inherited status electronics
(thanks to your electric supply,
they would not work.) Defunct showpieces!
And my tribal roots are dubious.

O you who earn like a dog
and eat like a horse!
It is true I own nothing,
nothing that will enhance my station,
and I may never own some things.
My bank balance is low,
almost non-existent.

I have acquired, on the other hand,
a cooking skill on my own,
I can make mint juleps, chow mein
and kheer.
I have acquired the habit of walking
and will not bow down to your polished god.
I can distinguish between a ghazal and a geet,
and I know something of the origin of blues,
a little of jazz and classical music.
I know something of medicine
and a doctor cannot dupe me just like that.
I believe in glasnost and the rastafa
and space colonisation.
I need not run from riches-starved virgins.
My friends believe in rock 'n' roll
and untangled sex. And in my profession
I'm not tyrannised by my boss, nor worry
of promotions and transfers.

I need not grease palms, nor sacrifice principles
when I profess none.

I can make love to women and improvise.
And when I kiss one we close our eyes—
while you grunt and ejaculate prematurely
within three minutes on your painted partner
as she smokes during the act perhaps
with a cigarette held between her toes.

Above all, no-one can remind me
of any Hippocratic oath.

A POEM FOR MOTHER

Palem Apokpi, mother who gave birth to me
how I hated leaving home, to be a man,
ten years ago. Now these hills
have grown on me.
But I'm still your shy son
with a voracious appetite,
the boy who lost many teeth
by emptying your larder
when you were away. And I'm
also your dreamy-eyed lad
who gave you difficult times
during his schooldays, running
after every girl he met, even
when he still wore half-pants.

You told your children

Money and Time do not grow on trees.
I haven't learnt how to use them well.
But it is not that I've forgotten
what you have come to mean to me.
Only I deserted much and left
so little of myself for others
to remember me at home.

I know how you toil as all mothers do
for unmarried sons and ageing husband
and liberated daughters-in-law.
Worried about us, for a long time
your lips couldn't blossom into a smile,
lines have furrowed your dear face and
the first signs of snow are on your hair.

Today, as on every day, you must have risen
with temple bells before cockcrow, swept
the floors and, after the ritual bath, cooked
for the remainder of us. I can see you
returning every day at dusk from the bazar,
your head laden with baskets.

Must you end thus toiling forever?

I'm sorry, Palem,
I've not inherited anything
of your gentle ways or culinary skills.
Forgive me, for all your dreams
of peace and rest during your remnant days,
I only turned out to be a small man,
with small dreams and living a small life.

THE MAWPHLANG SACRED GROVE

What follows is an extract from L.H. Pde's book *Ka Law Lyngdoh Mawphlang*, translated by the author and his daughter Loreta Kharmawphlang, which celebrates the Khasis' age-old green consciousness and the extraordinarily rich flora of their sacred groves, the biggest of which is at Mawphlang, the author's birthplace.

The sacred grove at Mawphlang, a heaven-sent treasure-house for environmentalists and botanists, is one of seven different kinds of grove to be found in the Chiefdom of Mawphlang.

Occupying a saucer-shaped depression, with hills falling away all round, this ancient forest is surrounded by numerous rough-hewn monoliths, erected in memory the departed Khasi elders. As you approach you'll see brightly clad Khasi women and girls, fetching water for domestic use, passing to and from the stream that meanders into the forest, with the usual conical basket on their backs, supported by a strap around the forehead.

As soon as you enter the grove you feel its cool air and a sense of refreshment that defies definition. You are in the humbling presence of Nature. Nothing may be removed from here: the ground is as soft as a carpet with the leaves and vegetation that has piled up, layer on layer, untouched through the ages. The entwining trees and orchids are so thick overhead that the sun's rays barely penetrate to the ferns, mosses, lichens and fungi on the forest floor.

The grove stands undisturbed today in its natural form not because of any legal sanction but because it is believed by the people that the sylvan deities would be offended were anything to be taken away, a belief reinforced by generations of oral tradition and by reference to the concept of the Basa, a village deity and guardian spirit of the grove. And Mawphlang, like any other sacred grove, also has its Suid Tynjang, a mischievous spirit who likes to confuse people. Such a spirit, it is claimed, used to haunt the Club House at Mawngap: whenever people forgot to light a fire, the spirit would come and harass them, and ask them to scratch his back.

Ever since I was a small boy, I have heard tales of the Basa. It comes, they say, in two forms, snake and tiger. If a person goes into the grove to do anything destructive, such as cutting grass for his pigs, the Basa will appear as a snake and position himself in the sty, so that the pig will not dare to venture inside. When people see such strange happenings, they begin to enquire where the grass came from. Then they say to the snake, "Go, please. They have done wrong and abused the grove." Then, as the people throw the grass back where it was taken from, the snake will disappear.

It is told that people who fail to repent in such circumstances may fall sick and even die. The story goes that once, not so long ago, a lady by the name of Thimur set out to visit a sick relative at Lyngkieñ. No-one, it seems, could diagnose his disease, and he was sinking fast. Finding a snake lying across her path, Thimur declared, "I'm going to visit my relative who is very ill. Please don't stand in my way." The snake would not move. Then a thought struck Thimur, and she said to the snake, "If my relative is ill becuase he has in some way abused the sacred forest, please let me go on so that I may admonish him." And the snake immediately disappeared. When Thimur reached Lyngkieñ she asked the sick man if he had disturbed the grove in any way, and he confessed that he had cut down some trees there. His family prayed and offered sacrifices of rice and water to appease the spirit—and the man recovered.

Then there was the time, about twenty years ago, when some airforce personnel went for a picnic at Madan Lyngktop, which is near the sacred grove. They fancied helping themselves to the many dry, fallen branches they could see in the forest, and started loading this firewood into their truck. The locals warned them that this was prohibited, but the airforce people paid them no attention. But the next day they returned, and carried back into the forest all the wood they had taken away, admitting to the bemused villagers that 'some strange things' had occurred in the night.

Ten years later the army came. They too loaded up their trucks with wood from the grove, careless of the warnings given by the locals. When they were set to drive away, their truck, although it had four-wheel drive, wouldn't budge. The confused army men unloaded half the wood, but still the vehicle wouldn't move. Not until they had unloaded every last twig did that truck move—suddenly, as if a chain had been released.

About fifteen years ago a man who had cut timber from the sacred grove exchanged the wood for some liquor, thinking that, having passed the wood on, nothing could possibly happen to him. But the Basa came in the form of a snake to the liquor-seller who had traded drink for wood, and demanded that what had been taken from the forest be returned. The liquor-seller, realising that the snake was the Basa, said that she, who had always respected the grove, would make enquiries and talk to the person who had violated it. She raised the matter with the man who had done the deal with her: he admitted his guilt and returned the wood to the forest. And that was the last that the liquor-seller saw of the snake.

Another strange incident befell the late Myntri (minister) Bonik Blah. At the time of the annual thanksgiving dance some wood was taken from the sacred grove and placed around the dancing ground. When the dance was over, the Myntri, assuming there was no further use for the timber, decided to use it for fencing his garden. The day his people brought the wood to his home, the Myntri's family noticed a snake in the house, and made to kill it. But Myntri Bonik stopped them, realising his error. "Go," he said to the snake, "I have done wrong and will return the wood." But the next day he forgot his promise, and the snake, returning to the house, and lay down on the Myntri's bed. The Myntri, overcome with fear, begged the snake's forgiveness and wasted no time, that very night, in returning the wood to the forest. After this he was left in peace.

Yes, the Basa is the guardian of the sacred grove, and he reminds people that anyone who behaves unscrupulously in the forest will be punished in strange ways, either physically or psychologically.

The locals also consider the Basa, in the form of a tiger, to be a guardian of innocent people. When suddenly, for some reason, people near the grove find themselves overcome with fear they may cry out "O Ni, O Kong, O Ryngkew, O Basa, please protect us from danger." Immediately, it is said, the characteristically gutteral sounds of the tiger, "khor, khor, khor", will be heard at their backs and the tiger's spirit felt on all sides. And when they consider that they are out of danger they may send the Basa away.

The rich flora and fauna of the Mawphlang sacred grove stand as testimony to the truth that preservation of Nature ensures the preservation of the human race, in both body and spirit. We humans are all hypocrites. We talk endlessly of doings things we have no intention of doing, while doing other things we'd rather not talk about. The cry for the preservation of forests is a cry in the wilderness. We depend too much on the government doing everything for us. And what right have we to preach, when we practise so little of what we preach? It would, nevertheless, be a very good thing if the District Council were to issue instructions to the Syiems (chieftains), the Lyngdohs (priests), the Sordars (headmen) and other administrators ordering the preservation of sacred groves.

Wise men say, "You may take a person from the forest but you cannot take the forest from a person." In about 1950, Israel, which had only just begun to stand on its own feet, was a desert barely fit for human habitation. Today, it is a leading nation in the world, thanks in no small measure to a law which stipulates that anyone caught felling a tree must plant two in its place. Another law provides that for every private occasion, such as weddings, a tree must be planted in memory of the event.

Here in Ri Khasi-Pnar, the land of the Khasi and Jaintia people, there are many species of trees, flowers, herbs, birds animals that have disappeared from our forests. Orchids even from the most sacred of our groves are turning up for sale in the city, in spite of a law against such practices. And where, all too often, are such orchids, animal hides and antlers to be found? Decorating the houses of the law-makers.

WEIKING*

I

Weiking, Weiking!
Spring is back, begin your whirling motions
and let our life live on.
Call your virgins to the circle,
let their gems and trinkets,
silks and velvet slap poverty in the face;
once in a year they must show us
all they have.
The drums beat, the flute sings,
let them begin their sleep-shuffling dance,
drifting round on white sand, bobbing
their gold and silver crowns in the sun.
Let young men as princes prance
in a ring, their silver swords flashing,
quivers jingling, as they pound
the earth chanting.
The devil take the rogue who dares break
that parapet of braves!

Whirl on, whirl on,
what if some of us
sneer at us for fools?
We are not here to pay obeisance
to the gods for a plentiful harvest
(do we ever have a harvest now?)
Whirl on, whirl on to a time
when women stood by their men
and men were tigers, guarding their homes
with jealous swords.

We who carry on the ways of our fathers
must protect our own.

II

I know a woman
who divorced her drunk
five years back,
only to carry a new belly
each year, because the drunk
returned to repent
whenever the belly was flat.

I know another one,
a quiet little girl
big with child,
looking for a job
as a maid . . .
Where is the husband?

III

Weiking, Weiking!
whirl on, whirl on,
our women are deserting us . . .

* *Weiking, meaning 'whirlpool', is a Khasi
dance enacted every spring. Virgin girls dance
slowly in the middle of a circular field, and
young men dance energetically around them, to
demonstrate that women are the keepers of the
home and men the protectors.*

THE INVITATION

However important or exciting
the invitation, it is always
with cold feet that I undertake
to leave these hills.

In a train death always seems to come
ripping like a ball in a cricket pitch.

Away from home
fear comes like a cringing dog.

CARTREFI PRYDLES YN SHILLONG

Yr anheddau sownd-wrth-ei-gilydd hyn
yw dedwydd gartrefi Shillong.
Mae'r trychfilod sy'n symud o'r naill
ystafell-rent i'r llall
yn goleuo'r agosatrwydd cyfoglyd
lle mae cyfrinachau nas croesewir,
ac a sibrydir yn y goslefau tyneraf,
yn ffrwydro fel ton o storom Cherra,
gan dabyrddu'n uchel-seinyddion yn y pen.

Genau'n cnoi a siaradant yn rhugl
am ddiosg eidion oddi ar esgyrn.
Anadliadau sydyn
a lefarant am fflam ambell lysieuyn poeth.
Crefu gwichlyd plant am ragor o gig
yn cwrdd â cherydd leddf y mamau,

50

cyfarwyddiadau parthed adfyd,
tystio'n llym a wnânt i ryddid llwm.

Clywir ac aroglir pob bytheiriad.
Mwmian a chwynfan,
rhan o rent tenantiaid i landlordiaid atgas,
cynllwynion maleisus ac anfri meddw,
tafell o drafodion cymdogol
a ridyllir drwy barwydydd main
i osod arnom undeb anesmwyth.

Sibrwd sercheiriau
a symudiadau rhythmig gwelyau dwbwl
yn uchel wichian yn nyfnder nos
a sbardunant ddelweddau Angelo
yng ngwres yr ymenydd.

Afiach, afiach yr agosatrwydd cyfoglyd hwn . . .
O am ddyrnaid o fyddardod!

ONLY MY TENANT

What if he is a professor?
What is he to me,
though he is an M. Phil or a doctorate?
I am the queen here,
the big-bosom queen.
And he, a mere tenant
to my high station in society.
Only a weed to me,
to be trampled and crushed

under my colourful high-heels.
Like this!
I can bitch him around too.
When he reads
I can turn on my cackling music,
beat my children
(so they cry),
or cut off his electric supply.
I can refuse him water
by which he rinses
his so-called learned mouth.

I can keep him in the common latrine
and deny him access to my private one
where my husband pours water every day
You see, he is nothing to me
but a little grasshopper.
Why should I treat him with respect
because he is a doctorate?
He is a nice man?
No, he is just afraid of my big mouth.

Maybe my husband is jobless now,
but he will get a job one day,
maybe after my fourth child, who knows?
You may condemn him for a lounger,
pestering the girls in the street
and holding the marijuana pipe in corners.
But if he says this is so,
they will have to agree, my tenants.
Let him beat me sometimes, so what?
That bloody professor might beat his wife too,
when he gets married;
or he might get drunk like my husband

and then I will laugh and say
serves you right for behaving like a saint.

But why do you praise only him?
Let him get his doctorate,
but don't doctorate with me.
I too am a doctor.
Maybe only a doctor of the beasts,
as you so uncharitably say,
but my tenants are my dogs:
if healthy, I give them shelter,
if mangy, I kick them out.

LINES WRITTEN TO MOTHERS WHO DISAGREE WITH THEIR SONS' CHOICES OF WOMEN

For managing to love
an object of scorn,
they place around my neck
a garland of threats.

And the world is cold this winter,
cold as the matrimonial column
they lecture to my sewn-shut ears,
or the stares that stalk
the woman of my choice.

But the cherries are pink
and festive as her love.

Leave cherries to winter, mother,
love to seasoned lovers.

THE PARKING LOT

I
The first ever Earth Summit
was given a big build-up for weeks,
almost like the death of Rajiv Gandhi.

In Rio
the world talks
of global warming
the ozone layer
pollution
and eroding rain forests.

At Nan Polok★
the parking lot
humbles down
fifteen of our proudest
pines.

II

There is a parking lot in Shillong
that took a year and lakhs to build.
Why, I asked, is it not used to ease congestion?
It awaits the Minister for Roads to inaugurate,
who awaits the fall of his government.
And the waiting goes on,
for here they change parties and governments
like Hindi film stars changing dresses in a song.

★ *Nan Polok: a lake and beauty spot in Shillong.*

ONLY STRANGE FLOWERS HAVE COME TO BLOOM

Since David Scott, they have come
a long way, these pears,* supplanting
the natives everywhere.

And charming, when spring returns,
their youthful forms, their
blossoms giving us such a sweet look.

In winter they seem starved
and stand despairing in the cold
having worked out their own misery.

Like them we shed our old ways
and having shed them we find
no spring to bring the flowers back.

For how long can we go on
living like wind-blown thistle down?

In the park I saw
those strange flowers again
that I have seen bossing around
courtyards and private gardens.

Like flowers, only strangers
and strange ways have come
to bloom in this land.

*Pears were first brought to the Khasi
Hills by David Scott, infamous British
'conquistador' of the region.*

WINTER SONG

Winter that sneaked into these hills
on the tenth moon has consolidated
its stay beyond the cherries.

Christmas like winter comes again and again
seducing our hearts with promises of heaven.

Life takes on a cheerfully, sneeringly
devout look, pines lose their limbs.
But the cunning dealer from the plains
does a brisk trade selling stars like *bindis.*★

This is the season for ecumenical blessings,
when neon lights and ornate pine limbs
make a home God-fearing.

When holly blooms from table cloths
and everything is silent for the songs
of the new-born king.

Must I never again hear the wind moan
from nocturnal silk strings?★★

The nights cavort with willing virgins
and virgin drinkers, singing hymns
in wobbly tones.

★ *Decorative dots worn on the foreheads of*
  Hindu women.
★★ *Traditional* duitara *music.*

GWENETH A. MAWLONG

A LADY

I knew a woman, a gracious lady
delivered from a natural birth.

She spoke in whispers, and her hair
of mighty waterfalls
was fragrant with earth and tendrils
and the breast-milk of pregnant hills.

In youth, her virginal body
was firm, inviting . . .
but she, on the threshold of her innocence,
was raped:

> men lusted,
> men penetrated,
> men battered.

She lives now all tangled up,
the thatched-roof home that once was hers
become a concreted harlot house.

She moans, shivers, cries aloud,
but few hear her, and fewer believe
her prayers will be answered,
her long-lost dream will be reborn,

this woman,
> my mother,
> > 'Meghalaya'.*

* *The state, founded in 1972, which the Khasi-Pnars share with the neighouring Garo tribe.*

57

RENDEZVOUS

Tall crystal glasses,
bamboo chair and table –
a well-furnished, one-room cabin.
Sitting on the edge of the sofa,
sipping fresh lemonade and crunching
crisp potato fingers,
I sigh deeply, I stretch my legs
their full length, ignoring
the slight sound of the creaking fabric
of my skin-tight faded blue jeans.

Reaching for his cigarette holder,
he moves lightly across the thick carpet.
I reach for my polythene bag
and, taking my cosmetics box,
rearrange my makeup carefully.
He watches me, says nothing,
not even teasing me
like he used to do . . .

Three years have gone by, and I
realise he has changed,
maybe I have too—
at least that leaves us
something to talk about.

FOR JERILEE

Aeons ago, lonely lady, aeons ago
I believe our lives touched.
You exist between yellow-stained
man-made pages, moulded and shaped
by human hands.
I exist in your shadow;
in my dark eyes, the reflection
of your tale.
Our voices in song
blend to perfection in a tune
that only you and I share.

Who, long-lost friends that we are,
who will drink to the falling stars?
The skyway has no need
of prodigies like us
who knew better than to lust
for straying animals.
Unlike you, Jerilee,
my pages are not numbered,
my life has no form
in letters, dates, words . . .
but, like you, I've grown older,
become ageless.

TO THE HILLS I KNOW

Sleep leads me, like waves lulling
my thoughts and oceanic yearnings,
leads me once again to a countryside
where cattle graze the tamed meadows
tended by shepherd boys
in ankle-length trousers
and cloaked in their check *tapmohkhlieh.**

My thoughts wander
by brooks and gushing falls,
shrubs, bushes, the sloping green
and a brown pathway leading to where
my lover and I will roam again,
seeking refuge in the pine groves
and tender grasses.

And I fall to musing

   how the golden reds of these hills
   mesh at twilight with the sky's blue linen,

   how my fathers witnessed
   the dawn of a paradise
   for nature's painters, earth's minstrels,

   how finely woven
   as the patterns of these hills
   are the stories that nourish us,
   the fables and legends,
   the living legend of U Tirot Singh**
   whose blood courses ageless
   through U Hynniewtrep.***

Soon I will return, soon I'll taste the dew
on the blossoming orchids, smell
the ripening pines and the red berries.
I will breathe again
the wintry lemon-scented air
and pass through sleepy smoking villages
with their laughing children.
And soon I'll be back
among the suburban intricacies
of that little town,
that sliver of heaven I call home.

* tapmohkhlieh: *a traditional shawl.*
** *U Tirot Singh: the Owain Glyndwr of the
Khasis who led a war of resistance against
the British.*
*** *U Hynniewtrep: 'the Seven Huts'.*

The Khasis, declares *The Dictionary of Welsh Biography* in an entry on Dr. John Roberts, "had no music of their own". It is a grotesque lie, symptomatic of the way in which the missionaries, sweepingly dismissive of 'backward' custom, encouraged their converts to look with shame and contempt on traditional Khasi culture.

It has long been recognised, even among Christians, that the powerful strictures of expansionist Presbyterianism did no small damage to Khasi folk culture—as of course they did, from the eighteenth century onwards, to the folk culture of Wales. Converts were obliged to dissociate themselves from all manifestations of 'erroneous' former ways and adopt not only a new religion but a new culture. The hymns of Pantycelyn and Ann Griffiths were to supplant the hypnotic drums and raucous *tangmuri* of the ancient rituals.

The most confident public manifestations of Khasi folk music are the drums and pipes of the big dance festivals, such as the Weiking Dance (see Kynpham Singh Nongkynrih's poem on p. ??) and the Nongkrem Dance. The five-day *Pomblang bad Shad Khyrim*, to give the latter its full name, is held every autumn in the village of Smit, some ten miles from Shillong. Smit is the headquarters of the Syiem, or chief, of Khyrim, the most proudly traditional of the twenty five Khasi states. Here, on a gritsand arena outside the Syiem's magnificent bow-backed palace, velvet-clad virgins shuffle back and forth, bare feet never leaving the ground, taut bodies moving only minimally to the music's insistent beat, while young men sweep around them, swirling swords and flicking silken whisks. The half dozen musicians play for five or six hours at a time, accompanying not only the dances, but the ritual eviscerations of roosters and the goat sacrifices. The snaking stridor of the oboe-like *tangmuri* has about it the blood-thrilling earthiness of vintage Beefheart. The

Nongkrem Dance is exuberant ceremonial art, with high religious purpose and deep social meaning.

The missionaries, of course, hated it—or, at best, affected disdain. Khasi dances in general, opined the Rev. Griffith Hughes in 1890, were characterised by "plenty of sound, but not a lot of music . . .. These dances, together with the archery competitions, represent the Khasis at their most barbarian. The language used by the boy dancers is lewd in the extreme." Until the missionaries left, it was an offence meriting instant banishment from the Church even to witness a traditional dance. Such anathemas are fading history by now, and there is considerable regret among Christians that so many families were persuaded to sell or melt down the crowns of silver and lariats of bobbled gold that were handed down over the generations for their daughters to wear in the dance.

Thousands of people attend these festivals, and there is considerable press coverage. But Khasi music has a quieter, lyrical side which, thanks to its more domestic expression, has suffered considerable neglect.

A leading exponent of this kind of music is Brek Wanswett, who, paradoxically, composed the song that rallied the peoples of Meghalaya behind a successful and bloodless campaign for full statehood. The exuberant "U Piad Khasi Baiar" has become a new national anthem, as popular as the Khasi version of "Hen Wlad Fy Nhadau".

Brek is master of the *duitara*, which is often referred to as 'the queen of Khasi instruments'. Vaguely akin to the guitar, the *duitara* has four silk strings, and is made of a single piece of hollowed-out papaya wood, with deerskin stretched over the soundbox. Its slightly muffled chatter is the perfect foil to his daughter Jurimon Risaw's blue sky of a voice.

It was the playing of these two fine musicians, in the BBC documentary *Monsoon* (1991), that first got me excited about the Khasis:

Hei ho u lapbah Sohra mynta u la wan.
Pangah dieng ki siej ba svmpat u Kyllan.
Her kynting lyoh khyndew na ki them sha ki lum . . .

[Hey! Here at last the torrential rains of Cherra./See the
whirlwind flay the swagger of trees and bamboos./Up fly the
clouds from earth to sky . . .]

Orchids, waterfalls, festivals, stones and sacred groves—Brek's
songs are hymns of praise to the beauty and endangered
customs of his treasured *Ri Khasi*.
A richly musical people, intensely fond of singing, the Khasis
took to the great Welsh hymns tunes as kites to a breeze—so
much so that, like the *hwyl* of Khasi oratory, the hymns are
now regarded as traditional; any move to 'indigenise' Christian
worship by introducing native instruments or compositions, as
advocated by certain youthful pastors, would run into stiff
resistance among older Presbyterians. But the musical genius of
someone such as Brek Wanswett could undoubtedly help the
Church to 'Khasify' its services.
When I visited Brek in Shillong, I put the 'indigenisation' idea
to him, but even he, being a Presbyterian, would have none of
what plainly struck him as a most unnatural proposition.
"Christ said, 'I build my church on rock, not on sand,'" he
declared. And that was an end to the matter.
Brek is acknowledged, by the few who take any serious
interest in the *duitara*, as one of the instrument's four or five
leading players.
"It was in 1960 that I started to play, in response to a music
competition. It was easier for me, because we attend the
church and we sing tonic sol-fa—although in those days, of
course, the church discouraged the playing of traditional
instruments. But in the late 'sixties the church started relaxing
its attitude."

If congregations remain conservatively attached to the Welsh hymns, official disapproval of indigenous music has now evaporated. The Presbyterian Church has recently decided to establish a cultural department which may be in a position to give Brek and others the support that has been sadly lacking.

Meghalaya's state radio seems to be the only organisation in the Khasi Hills promoting Khasi music, although the paltry two rupees (four pence) royalty paid for a new piece of music is not enough to keep a musician in *duitara* strings. In Brek Wanswett, Jurimon Risaw, Sanjarawaiñ Risaw, and musicians like them, Khasi culture (not to mention the authorities responsible for promoting tourism) has assets which it is wastefully squandering. Church and classical music, Hindi and western pop have deafened people's ears to the sounds of their own culture.

"Traditionally," said Brek, "the public expectation of playing and enjoying Khasi music is bound up only with the dance. The *duitara*, though, is used in little story-telling gatherings around the hearth. And the flute is used by the shepherds in the fields. There's no regular appreciation, no professional connection in the application of our music. It's just for our own satisfaction, a little bit of recreation after a hard day's work.

"You'll find that a lot of Khasi stories are tales—often told to music—about how to grow up, because the parents, busy all day in the fields, don't always have time to teach their children in any other way.

"Why do youngsters lose interest and get attracted to Indian or Western music? Because, until now, there have been no artists among us playing their own instruments to international standards. If there was somebody to play our own music and cross the barrier of the Khasi Hills and Meghalaya, our people would be attracted to their own music.

"Another problem is that all educated and learned musicians

live in Shillong, and Shillong is steeped in classical, church, jazz and pop music. Those people who know our traditional music can't write it down, they are village people. And the town people, who could write it down, don't go to the villages, they tend to ignore traditional music."

As the author of the only Khasi musical text book in existence, Brek hopes that more tonic sol-fa transcriptions will help popularise the music, but the breakthrough he hopes for is unlikely to happen until someone with vision, and a modest amount of money, begins to make discs and tapes of this music.

"There is a need to get our music recognised," he said. "The idea of playing our music and celebrating our culture in case it goes away has not entered the public mind."

No recording of traditional Khasi music is publicly available, although before I left Shillong, Brek kindly presented me with a one-off compilation of bits and pieces he had recorded either in the home or in the studio, for the state radio station. He described them too modestly as "recorded in raw stage": most are recorded to a high standard, and are crying out for the wider distribution that is secured only by commercial publication. Let's hope that by the time Brek & co. leave the *gwlad beirdd and chantorion* some enterprising folk label will have offered them a contract.

BIOGRAPHIES OF THE MUSICIANS

BREK WANSWETT (b. 1935) has been making music since his choirboy days in the village church. He started composing in 1952, and has written and published scores of songs, some of which have attained the status of people's anthems. A teacher of music and the winner of many prizes, he has taken Khasi music all over India, and broadcasts regularly. His music featured on the BBC documentary *Monsoon* (1991) and figured prominently in the films made by Teliesyn for S4C and the BBC, *Gwalia yng Nghasia* (1994) and *Gwalia in Khasia* (1995).

JURIMON RISAW (b. 1964), Brek Wanswett's daughter, featured alongside her father in both *Monsoon* and the Teliesyn films. She also sings regularly on Indian radio and television, and works as a librarian for All India Radio, Shillong. As a gospel singer, she toured India with the Jubilee Messengers in 1987.

SANJARAWAIÑ RISAW (b. 1972), Brek Wanswett's son, is a percussionist, often with his father and sister, in a number of traditional music groups. He too featured in the Teliesyn films, and has appeared on local and national radio and television, sometimes playing the guitar. He is a student in Shillong.